ROOSTERS

BY MILCHA SANCHEZ-SCOTT

**DRAMATISTS
PLAY SERVICE
INC.**

ABOUT THE AUTHOR

The daughter of a Colombian father and an Indonesian mother, Milcha Sanchez-Scott was born on the island of Bali in 1954. She was educated in England until her early teens, when her family emigrated to California. A graduate of the University of San Diego, Sanchez-Scott lives in Los Angeles. Her first play *Latina*, premiered by L.A. Theatre Works in 1980, won seven *Drama-Logue* awards. *Dog Lady* and *The Cuban Swimmer*, a pair of one-acts written in 1982, were produced in 1984 by INTAR in New York, and selected for TCG's *Plays in Process* series. *Dog Lady* was subsequently published in *Best Plays of 1986*. Current works in progress include *City of Angels*, a trio of one-acts; *Evening Star*, to be produced by New York's Theatre for a New Audience in the spring; and *Paper Wedding*, a piece being created at Los Angeles Theatre Center.

Sanchez-Scott has received the Vesta Award, given each year to a West Coast woman artist, and the Le Compte du Noüy Foundation Award, which goes to "a young writer with a unique voice." She holds a First Level Award for American playwrights from the Rockefeller Foundation for 1987.

ROOSTERS was presented by Intar (Max Ferrá, Artistic Director; Dennis Ferguson-Acosta, Managing Director) and the New York Shakespeare Festival (Joseph Papp, Producer) at Intar in New York City on March 11, 1987. It was directed by Jackson Phippin; the set was by Loy Arcenas; the lighting was by John Gisondi; the costumes were by C.L. Hundley; the sound was by Janet Kalas; the fight direction was by Nels Hennum; the dialect consultant was Tim Monich; and the stage manager was Michele Steckler. The cast was as follows:

GALLO............................Joaquim De Almeida

HECTOR ....Joanathan Del Arco

ANGELA...................................Sara Erde

JUANA...............................Suzanne Costallos

CHATA ....Ilka Tanya Payan

ADAN...................................Albert Farrar

THE CHARACTERS

Gallo

Zapata

Hector

Angela

Juana

Chata

Adan

Shadow #1

Shadow #2

San Juan

TIME

The present.

PLACE

The Southwest.

ROOSTERS

ACT ONE

Scene 1

Stage and house are dark. Slowly a narrow pinspot of light comes up. We hear footsteps. Enter Gallo, a very, very handsome man in his forties. He is wearing a cheap dark suit, with a white open-neck shirt. He carries a suitcase. He puts the suitcase down. He faces the audience.

GALLO. Lord Eagle, Lord Hawk, sainted ones, spirits and winds, Santa Maria Aurora of the Dawn ... I want no resentment, I want no rancor .... I had an old red Cuban hen. She was squirrel-tailed and sort of slab-sided and you wouldn't have given her a second look. But she was a queen. She could be thrown with any cock and you would get a hard-kicking stag every time. I had a vision, of a hard-kicking flyer, the ultimate bird. The Filipinos were the ones with the pedigree Bolinas, the high flyers, but they had no real kick. To see those birds fighting in the air like dark avenging angels ... well like my father use to say, "Son nobles ... finos...." I figured to mate that old red Cuban. This particular Filipino had the best. A dark burgandy flyer named MacArther. He wouldn't sell. I began borrowing MacArthur at night, bringing him back before dawn, no one the wiser, but one morning the Filipino's son caught me. He pulled out his blade. I pulled out mine. I was faster. I went up on manslaughter.... They never caught on ... thought I was in the henhouse trying to steal their stags.... It took time — refining, inbreeding, cross-breeding, brother to sister, mother to son, adding power, rapid attack ... but I think we got him. *(Gallo stands still for a beat, checks his watch, takes off his jacket and faces C. A slow, howling drumbeat begins. As it gradually goes higher in pitch and excitement mounts, we see narrow beams of light, the first light of dawn, filtering through chicken wire. The light reveals a heap of chicken feathers which turns out to be an actor/dancer who represents the rooster Zapata. Zapata stretches his wings, then his neck, to greet the light. He stands and struts proudly, puffs his chest and crows his salutation to the sun. Gallo stalks Zapata, as drums follow their movements.)* Ya, ya, mi lindo ... yeah, baby ... you're a beauty, a real beauty. Now let's see whatcha got. *(He pulls out a switchblade stiletto. It gleams in the light as he tosses it from hand to hand.)* Come on baby boy. Show Daddy whatcha got. *(Gallo lunges at Zapata. Zapata parries with his beak and wings. This becomes a slow, rhythmic fight-dance. Gallo grabs Zapata by his comb, bending his head backwards until he is forced to sit. Gallo stands behind Zapata, straddling him. With one hand Gallo holds Zapata's comb, with the other he holds the knife next to Zapata's neck.)* Oh yeah, you like to fight? Huh? You gonna kill for me baby boy? Huh? *(Gallo sticks the tip of the knife into Zapata. The rooster squawks in pain.)* Sssh! Baby boy, you gotta learn. Daddy's gotta teach you. *(Gallo sticks it to Zapata again. This time the rooster snaps back in anger.)* That's right beauty ... Now you got it ... Come on, come. *(Gallo waves his knife and hand close to Zapata's face. The rooster's head and eyes follow.)* Oh yeah ... that's it baby, take it! Take it! *(Suddenly Zapata attacks, drawing blood. Gallo's body contracts in orgasmic pleasure/pain. Loudly.)* Ay precioso! ... Mi lindo ... You like that, eh? Taste good, huh? *(Gallo waves the gleaming knife in a slow hypnotic movement which calms the rooster.)* Take my blood, honey ... I'm in you now ... Morales blood, the blood of kings ... and you're my rooster ... a Morales rooster. *(He slowly backs away from the rooster. He picks up his suitcase, still pointing the knife at Zapata.)* Kill. You're my son. Make me proud. *(Gallo exits. Zapata puffs his chest and struts U. Lights go up a little on U. L. area as the rooster goes into the chicken-wire henhouse. He preens and scratches. Enter Hector, a young man of about twenty. He is very handsome. He wears gray sweatpants and no shirt. On his forehead is a sweatband. His hair and body are dripping wet. He has been running. Now he is panting as he leans on the henhouse looking at Zapata.)*

HECTOR. I saw what you did to those chicks. Don't look at me like you have a mind, or a soul, or feelings. You kill your young ... and we are so proud of your horrible animal vigor ... But you are my inheritance ... Abuelo's gift to me ... to get me out. Oh, Abuelo, Grandfather ... you should have left me your courage, your sweet pacific strength. *(A ray of light hits D.R. In a semi-shadow, we see a miniature cemetery, with small white headstones and white crosses. We see the profile of a young angel/girl with wings and a pale dress. Angela is kneeling next to a bare desert tree with low scratchy branches. She has a Buster Brown haircut and a low tough voice. She is fifteen, but looks twelve.)*
ANGELA. *(Loudly.)*
Angel of God
My Guardian Dear
To whom God's love
Commits me here
Ever this day be
At my side
To light and guard
To rule and guide
Amen.
(Her paper wings get caught in a tree branch.) Aw, shit! *(She exits.)*

Scene 2

As the light changes we hear the clapping of women making tortillas. Lights come up full. Center is a faded wood-frame house, with a porch that is bare except for a table and a few chairs. The house sits in the middle of a desert agricultural valley somewhere in the Southwest. Everything is sparse. There is a feeling of blue skies and space. One might see off on the horizon tall Nopales or Century cactus. Juana, a thin, wornout-looking

9

woman of thirty-five, comes out of the house. She is wearing a faded housedress. She goes to mid-yard, faces front and stares out.

JUANA. It's dry. Bone dry. There's a fire in the mountains ... up near Jacinto Pass. *(The clapping stops for a beat, then continues. Juana starts to go back into the house, then stops. She sniffs the air, sniffs again, and again.)* Tres Rosas ... I smell Tres Rosas. *(She hugs her body and rocks.)* Tres Rosas ... Ay, St. Anthony let him come home ... Let him be back. *(The clapping stops. Chata enters from the house. She is a fleshy woman of forty, who gives new meaning to the word blowsy. She has the lumpy face of a hard boozer. She walks with a slight limp. She wears a black kimono, on the back of which if embroidered in red a dragon and the words "Korea, U.S.S. Perkins, 7th Fleet." A cigarette hangs from her lips. She carries a bowl containing balls of tortilla dough.)* I smell Tres Rosas ... The brilliantine for his hair ... He musta been here. Why did he go?

CHATA. Men are shit.

JUANA. Where could he be?

CHATA. First day out of jail! My brother never comes home first day. You should know that. Gotta sniff around ... gotta get use to things. See his friends.

JUANA. Sí, that's right ... He just gotta get used to things. I'll feel better when I see him ... I gotta keep busy.

CHATA. You been busy all morning.

JUANA. I want him to feel good, be proud of us ... You hear anything when you come in yesterday?

CHATA. Who's gonna know anything at the Trailways bus station?

JUANA. You ain't heard anything?

CHATA. Juanita, he knows what he's doing. If there was gonna be any trouble he'd know. Ay, mujer, he's just an old warrior coming home.

JUANA. Ain't that old.

CHATA. For a fighting man, he's getting up there. *(Juana slaps tortillas. Chata watches her.)* Who taught you to make tortillas?

JUANA. I don't remember. I never make 'em. Kids don't ask.
CHATA. Look at this. You call this a tortilla? Have some pride. Show him you're a woman.
JUANA. Chata, you've been here one day, and you already—
CHATA. Ah, you people don't know what it is to eat fresh handmade tortillas. My grandmother Hortensia, the one they used to call "La India Condenada" ... she would start making them at five o'clock in the morning. So the men would have something to eat when they went into the fields. Hijo! She was tough ... Use to break her own horses ... and her own men. Every day at five o'clock she would wake me up. "Buenos pinchi días," she would say. I was twelve or thirteen years old, still in braids ... "Press your hands into the dough," "Con fuerza," "Put your stamp on it." One day I woke up, tú sabes, con la sangre. "Ah! So you're a woman now. Got your cycle like the moon. Soon you'll want a man, well this is what you do. When you see the one you want, you roll the tortilla on the inside of your thigh and then you give it to him nice and warm. Be sure you give it to him and nobody else." Well, I been rolling tortillas on my thighs, on my nalgas, and God only knows where else, but I've been giving my tortillas to the wrong men ... and that's been the problem with my life. First there was Emilio. I gave him my first tortilla. Ay Mamacita, he use to say, these are delicious. Aye, he was handsome, a real lady-killer! After he did me the favor he didn't have the cojones to stick around ... took my TV set too. They're all shit ... the Samoan bartender, what was his name...
JUANA. Nicky, Big Nicky.
CHATA. The guy from Pep Boys—
JUANA. Chata, you really think he'll be back?
CHATA. His son's first time in the pit? With "the" rooster? A real Morales rooster? Honey, he'll be back. Stop worrying.
JUANA. Let's put these on the griddle. Angela, Hector ... breakfast.

Scene 3

Angela slides out from under the house, wearing her wings. She carries a white box which contains her cardboard tombstones, paper and crayons, a writing tablet and a pen. She too sniffs the air. She runs to the little cemetery and looks up, as Hector appears at the window behind her.

ANGELA. Tres Rosas ... Did you hear? Sweet Jesus, Abuelo, Queen of Heaven, all the Saints, all the Angels. It is true. It is certain. He is coming, coming to stay forever and ever. Amen.

HECTOR. Don't count on it!

ANGELA. *(To Heaven.)* Protect me from those of little faith and substance.

HECTOR. I'm warning you. You're just going to be disappointed.

ANGELA. *(To Heaven.)* Guard me against the enemies of my soul.

HECTOR. Your butt's getting bigger and bigger!

ANGELA. And keep me from falling in with low companions.

HECTOR. Listen, little hummingbird woman, you gotta be tough, and grown-up today. *(Angela digs up her collection can and two dolls. Both dolls are dressed in nuns' habits. One, the St. Lucy doll, has round sunglasses. She turns a box over to make a little tea table on which she places a doll's teapot and cups.)*

ANGELA. As an act of faith and to celebrate her father's homecoming, Miss Angela Ester Morales will have a tea party.

HECTOR. No more tea parties.

ANGELA. Dancing in attendance will be that charming martyr St. Lucy.

HECTOR. He will not be impressed.

12

ANGELA. Due to the loss of her eyes and the sensitivity of her alabaster skin, St. Lucy will sit in the shade. *(She sits St. Lucy in the shade and picks up the other doll.)*

HECTOR. Who's that?

ANGELA. St. Teresa of Avigon, you will sit over here. *(She seats St. Teresa doll.)*

HECTOR. Just don't let him con you Angela.

ANGELA. *(Pouring pretend tea.)* One lump or two, St. Lucy? St. Teresa has hyperglycemia, and only takes cream in her tea. Isn't that right St. Teresa?

HECTOR. He's not like Abuelo. *(Angela animates the dolls like puppets and uses two different voices as St. Lucy and St. Teresa.)*

ANGELA. *(As St. Teresa.)* Shouldn't we wait for St. Luke?

HECTOR. Stop hiding. You can't be a little girl forever.

ANGELA. *(As St. Lucy.)* St. Luke! St. Luke! Indeed! How that man got into Heaven I'll never know. That story about putting peas in his boots and offering the discomfort up to God is pure bunk. I happen to know he boiled the peas first.

HECTOR. I don't want you hurt. It's time to grow up.

ANGELA. *(As St. Teresa.)* St. Lucy! I can only think that it is the loss of your eyes that makes you so disagreeable. Kindly remember that we have all suffered to be saints.

HECTOR. Are you listening to me, Angie?

ANGELA. *(As St. Lucy.)* Easy for you to say! They took my eyes because I wouldn't put out! They put them on a plate. A dirty, chipped one, thank you very much indeed! To this day no true effort has been made to find them.

HECTOR. Excuse me! ... Excuse me, St. Teresa, St. Lucy, I just thought I should tell you ... a little secret ... your hostess, Miss Angela Ester Morales, lies in her little, white, chaste, narrow bed, underneath the crucifix, and masturbates.

ANGELA. Heretic! Liar!

HECTOR. Poor Jesus, up there on the cross, right over her bed, his head tilted down. He sees everything.

ANGELA. Lies! Horrible lies!

HECTOR. Poor saint of the month, watching from the night table.

13

ANGELA. I hate you! I hate you! Horrible, horrible, Hector.

JUANA. *(From offstage.)* Breakfast! *(Hector leaves the window. Angela sits on the ground writing on a tombstone.)*

ANGELA. *(Lettering tombstone.)* Here lies Horrible Hector Morales. Died at age twenty, in great agony, for tormenting his little sister.

JUANA. *(Offstage.)* You kids ... breakfast!

HECTOR. *(Pops up at window.)* Just be yourself. A normal sex-crazed fifteen-year-old girl with a big gigantic enormous butt. *(He exits.)*

ANGELA. *(To Heaven.)*
Send me to Alaska
Let me be frozen
Send me a contraction
A shrinking antidote
Make me little again
Please make my legs
Like tiny pink Vienna sausages
Give me back my little butt.

(Juana and Chata bring breakfast out on the porch and set it on the table.)

JUANA. Angie! Hector! We ain't got all day. *(Angela goes to the breakfast table with the St. Lucy doll and the collection can.)* And take your wings off before you sit at the table. Ain't you kids got any manners? *(Angela removes her wings, sits down, bows her head in prayer. Chata stares at St. Lucy. St. Lucy stares at Chata. Juana shoos flies and stares at the distant fire.)* I hope he's on this side of the fire.

CHATA. That doll's staring at me.

ANGELA. She loves you. *(Lights fade on the women, come up on the henhouse. Adan, a young man of twenty, is talking to Zapata — now a real rooster, not the actor/dancer — and preparing his feed.)*

ADAN. Hola Zapata ... ya mi lindo ... mi bonito. En Inglés. Tengo que hablar en English ... pinchi English ... verdad Zapata? En Español más romántico pero Hector say I must learned di English. *(Zapata starts squawking.)* Qué te pasa? Orita vas a comer.

14

(Hector enters.)
HECTOR. English, Adan ... English.
ADAN. No English ... pinchi English.
HECTOR. Good morning, Adan.
ADAN. A que la fregada! ... Okay this morning in the fields, I talk English pero this afternoon for fight I talk puro Español.
HECTOR. Good morning, Adan.
ADAN. Sí, sí, good morning, muy fine ... Hector el Filipino he say ... *(He moves away from Zapata, so bird will not hear him.)* He say to tell you que Zapata no win. Porque Filipino bird fight more y your bird first fight y your first fight y you not no ex ... ex...
HECTOR. Experience.
ADAN. Sí eso, he say you sell bird to him y no fight ... He say is not true Morales bird porque Gallo not here. El Filipino say if you fight bird ... bird dead. If bird still alive after Filipino bird beat him ... Bird still dead porque nobody pay money for bird that lose.
HECTOR. But if he wins, everybody wants him.
ADAN. I say, ay di poor Hector. His abuelo leave him bird. He can no sell. El Filipino say, "Good!" Inside, in my heart I am laughing so hard porque he not know Gallo gonna be here. We win, we make much money.
HECTOR. It's my bird, I have to do it myself.
ADAN. You tonto! You stupido! You mulo! Like donkey ... He help you, he the king ... he you papa. For him all birds fight.
HECTOR. No!
ADAN. Why? Why for you do this? You no even like bird. Zapata he knows this, he feel this thing in his heart. You just want money to go from the fields, to go to the other side of the mountains ... to go looking to go looking for what? On the other side is only more stupid people like us.
HECTOR. How could you think I just wanted money? I want him to see me.
ADAN. Sorry ... I am sorry my friend ... I know ... I stay with you y we win vas a ver! Okay Zapata! We win y est a noche estamos tomando Coors, Ripple, Lucky Lager, unas Buds, Johnny Walkers, oh sí, y las beautiful señoritas. *(He gives Zapata his food.)* Eat

15

Zapata! Be strong.

HECTOR. I almost forgot, look what I have for you ... fresh, warm homemade tortillas.

ADAN. Oh, how nice.

HECTOR. Yes, how nice. Aunt Chata made them.

ADAN. Oh, much nice.

HECTOR. Today she woke up at five o'clock, spit a green booger the size of a small frog into a wad of Kleenex. She wrapped her soiled black "7th Fleet" kimono around her loose, flaccid, tortured, stretch-marked body and put her fat-toed, corned yellow hooves into a pair of pink satin slippers. She slap-padded over to the sink where she opened her two hippo lips and looked into the mirror. She looked sad. I looked at those lips ... those lips that had wrapped themselves warmly and lovingly around the cocks of a million campesinos, around thousands upon thousands of Mexicanos, Salvadoreños, Guatemaltecos. For the tide of brown men that flooded the fields of this country, she was there with her open hippo whore's lips, saying "Bienvenidos," "Welcome," "Hola," "Howdy." Those are legendary lips, Adan.

ADAN. Yes ... muy yes.

HECTOR. What a woman, what a comfort. Up and down the state in her beat-up station wagon. A '56 Chevy with wood panels on the sides, in the back a sad, abused mattress. She followed the brown army of pickers through tomatoes, green beans, zucchinis, summer squash, winter squash, oranges, and finally Castroville, the artichoke capital of the world, where her career was stopped by the fists of a sun-crazed compañero. The ingratitude broke her heart.

ADAN. Oh my gooseness!

HECTOR. She was a river to her people, she should be rewarded, honored. No justice in the world.

ADAN. Pinchi world. *(He and Hector look to mountains.)* You look mountains. In my country I look mountains to come here. I am here and everybody still look mountains.

HECTOR. I want to fly right over them.

ADAN. No, my friend, we are here, we belong ... la tierra.

16

JUANA. *(From offstage.)* Hector, I ain't calling you again. *(Light up on the porch. Juana and Chata are sitting at the table. Angela is sitting on the steps. She has her wings back on. St. Lucy and the collection can are by her side. She is writing on her tablet.)* Oh Gallo, what's keeping you?

CHATA. Men are shit! That's all. And it's Saturday. When do they get drunk? When do they lose their money? When do they shoot each other? Saturdays, that's when the shit hits the fan. *(Enter Hector and Adan with Zapata in a traveling carrier.)*

JUANA. It's because I'm so plain.

HECTOR. We're better off without him.

CHATA. Buenos días Adan. Un cafecito?

ADAN. Ah. Good morning, Mrs. Chata, no gracias, ah good morning, Mrs. Morales y Miss Angelita. *(Angela sticks out her donation can. Adan automatically drops coins in.)*

JUANA. Angela!

ADAN. No, is good, is for the poor. Miss Angela, she good lady ... eh, girl. *(He pats Angela on the head.)*

JUANA. Why don't you leave the bird, so your father can see him when he gets home.

HECTOR. He's my bird. He can see it later.

JUANA. I can't believe you would do this to your own father. Birds are his life ... and he's so proud of you.

HECTOR. This is news. How would he know, he hasn't seen me in years.

JUANA. It isn't his fault.

HECTOR. It never is.

JUANA. Your father is with us all the time, he got his eye on us, he knows everything we're doing.

ANGELA. Everything!

JUANA. I brag about you kids in my letters ... His friends they tell him what a smart boy you are ... that you're good-looking like him ... He's proud ... "A real Morales," that's what he says.

HECTOR. And did he call me a winner? A champ? A prince? And did you tell him I was in the fields?

ANGELA. What did he say about me, Mama?

HECTOR. Nothing, you're a girl and a retard. What possible use could he have for you? Grow up!

CHATA. No, you grow up. *(Angela buries herself in Chata's lap.)*

JUANA. Hector, please, Hector, for me.

HECTOR. No, Mother. Not even for you.

JUANA. You give him a chance.

HECTOR. What chance did he give us? Fighting his birds, in and out of trouble. He was never here for us, never a card, a little present for Angela. He forgot us.

JUANA. You don't understand him. He's different.

HECTOR. Just make it clear to him. Abuelo left the bird to me, not to him, to me.

JUANA. Me, me, me. You gonna choke on this me, me. Okay, okay, I'm not going to put my nose in the bird business. I just ask you for me, for Angie, be nice to him.

HECTOR. As long as we all understand the "bird business," I'll be nice to him even if it kills me, Mother.

JUANA. Now you're feeling sorry for yourself. Just eat. You can feel sorry for yourself later.

HECTOR. Why didn't I think of that. I'll eat now and feel sorry for myself later.

JUANA. Now, you kids gotta be nice and clean, your papa don't like dirty people.

CHATA. Me too, I hate dirty people.

JUANA. Angie, you take a bath.

HECTOR. Oh, Angela, how ... how long has it been since you and water came together? *(Angela hits him.)* Oww!

JUANA. You put on a nice clean dress, and I don't wanna see you wearing no dirty wings.

HECTOR. Right, Angie, put on the clean ones.

JUANA. You say please and excuse me ... and you watch your table manners ... I don't want to see any pigs at my table.

HECTOR. *(Making pig noises.)* What a delicious breakfast! Cold eggs, sunny-side up. How cheery! How uplifting! Hmm, hmmm! *(He turns so Angela can see him. He picks up the eggs with his hands and stuffs them in his mouth.)* Look, Angela, refried beans in a delicate pool of congealed fat. *(Still making pig noises, he picks up gobs of beans, stuffs them into his mouth.)*

CHATA. A que la fregada! Hector, stop playing with your food. You're making us sick.

JUANA. *(Looking at watch.)* 7:20, you got ten minutes before work. *(Hector drums his fingers on the table.)*

HECTOR. Nine minutes ... I will now put on the same old smelly, shit-encrusted boots, I will walk to the fields. The scent of cow dung and rotting vegetation will fill the air. I will wait with the same group of beaten-down, pathetic men ... taking their last piss against a tree, dropping hard warm turds in the bushes. All adding to this fertile whore of a valley. At 7:30 that yellow mechanical grasshopper, the Deerfield tractor, will belch and move. At this exact moment, our foreman, John Knipe, will open his pig-sucking mouth, exposing his yellow, pointy, plaque-infested teeth. He yells, "Start picking, boys." The daily war begins ... the intimidation of violent growth ... the expanding melons and squashes, the hardiness of potatoes, the waxy purple succulence of eggplant, the potency of ripening tomatoes. All so smug, so rich, so ready to burst with sheer generosity and exuberance. They mock me ... I hear them ... "Hey Hector," they say, "show us whatcha got," and "Yo Hector we got bacteria out here more productive than you." ... I look to the ground. Slugs, snails, worms slithering in the earth with such ferocious hunger they devour their own tails, flies oozing out larvae, aphids, bees, gnats, caterpillars their prolification only slightly dampened by our sprays. We still find eggsacks hiding, ready to burst forth. Their teeming life, their lust, is shameful ... Well it's time ... Bye Ma. *(He exits.)*

JUANA. *(Yelling.)* Hector! You gotta do something about your attitude. *(To herself.)* Try to see the bright side. *(Juana and Chata exit into the house, leaving Angela on the porch steps. Adan runs up to her.)*

ADAN. Psst! Miss Angelita! ... di ... di cartas?

ANGELA. Oh, the letters ... that will be one dollar.

ADAN. One dollar! Adan very poor man ... *(Angela sticks the dona-*

19

tion can out and shakes it. Adan reaches into his pockets and drops coins into the can.) Oh, sí, you are very good. *(Angela puts on glasses and pulls out a letter.)*

ANGELA. *(Reading letter.)* Adored Señora Acosta: The impulses of my heart are such that they encourage even the most cautious man to commit indiscretion. My soul is carried to the extreme with the love that only you could inspire. Please know that I feel a true passion for your incomparable beauty and goodness. I tremulously send this declaration and anxiously await the result. Your devoted slave, Adan.

ADAN. *(Sighing.)* Ay, que beautiful.

ANGELA. P.S. With due respect Señora, if your husband should be home, do not turn on the porch light.

ADAN. Ah, thank you ... thank you very much. *(Adan hurriedly exits. Angela gathers her St. Lucy doll and her donation can, and exits quickly. Chata enters from the house wearing "colorful" street clothes. She looks around, then swiftly exits. Hector enters, picks up Zapata, hurries off. The stage darkens, as if smoke from the distant fire has covered the sun. Drum howls are heard. In the distance we hear a rooster crow and sounds of excited chickens as the henhouse comes to life. Gallo appears.)*

GALLO. Easy hens, shshsh! My beauties. *(He puts his suitcase down, cups his hands to his mouth, and yells to the house.)* Juana! Juana! Juana! *(Juana opens the door.)* How many times, in the fever of homesickness, have I written out that name on prison walls, on bits of paper, on the skin of my arms ... Let me look at you ... my enduring rock, my anchor made from the hard parts of the earth — minerals, rocks, bits of glass, ground shells, the brittle bones of dead animals.

JUANA. I never seen you so pale, so thin...

GALLO. I'm home to rest, to fatten up, to breathe, to mend, to you.

JUANA. How long? How long will you stay?

GALLO. Here. Here is where I'll put my chair ... I will sit here basking in the sun, like a fat old iguana catching flies, and watching my grandchildren replant the little cemetery with the bones of tiny sparrows. Here. Here I will build the walks for my champions. Morales roosters. The brave and gallant red Cubans, the hard and high-kicking Irish Warhorses, the spirited high-flying Bolinas.

JUANA. Don't say nothing you don't mean ... you really gonna stay?

GALLO. *(Gently.)* Here. Here is where I'll plant a garden of herbs. Blessed laurel to cure fright, wild marjoram for the agony of lovesickness, cempauchie flowers for the grief of loneliness. *(Gallo gently kisses Juana, picks her up and carries her into the house. The door slams shut. Angela enters, her wings drooping behind her. She trips over Gallo's suitcase. She examines it. She smells it.)*

ANGELA. Tres Rosas! *(Angela looks at the house. She sits on the suitcase, crosses her arms over her chest as if she were ready to wait an eternity. The shadows of two strangers fall on her.)* What do you want?

SHADOW #1. Nobody's home to you, rancor.

SHADOW #2. Just go in, tell him we got something for him.

ANGELA. Nobody's home to you, resentment.

SHADOW #1. Who are you supposed to be?

ANGELA. *(Holding St. Lucy doll.)*

I am the angel of this yard
I am the angel of this door
I am the angel of light
I am the angel who shouts
I am the angel who thunders

SHADOW #1. She is pure crazy.

SHADOW #2. Don't play with it, it's serious.

ANGELA.

You are the shadow of resentment
You are the shadow of rancor
I am the angel of acid saliva
I will spit on you.

SHADOW #1. There's time.

SHADOW #2. Yeah, later. *(Angela spits. The shadows leave. Angela crosses her hands over her chest and looks to Heaven.)*

ANGELA. Holy Father ... Listen, you don't want him, you want me. Please take me, claim me, launch me and I will be your shoot-

21

ing star woman. I will be your comet woman. I will be your morning-star woman.

Scene 4

Lights become brighter. Angela exits under the house. The door opens. Gallo comes out in T-shirt and pants and goes to his suitcase. Juana comes to the door in slip and tight robe.

GALLO. I never sent him to the fields.

JUANA. I know.

GALLO. I never said for you to put him there.

JUANA. No, you never said...

GALLO. Then why is my son in the fields? *(They look at each other. Gallo looks away.)* Don't look at me. I see it in your eyes. You blame me. Just like the old man.

JUANA. Abuelo never said a word against you.

GALLO. I never let him down with the birds, nobody could match me. They were the best.

JUANA. He knew that...

GALLO. So, he left the bird to Hector.

JUANA. He wanted him out of the fields. We didn't know when you would be out or maybe something would happen to you.

GALLO. He let the boy into the fields, that was his sin. He allowed a Morales into the fields.

JUANA. He was old, tired, heartbroken.

GALLO. Heartbroken, he wasn't a woman to be heartbroken.

JUANA. His only son was in jail.

GALLO. Yes, we know that, the whole valley knows that. You... what did you do? Didn't you lay out your hard, succulent, bitch's teat at the breakfast table? So he would have the strength to stand behind a hoe, with his back bent and his eyes on the mud for ten hours a day.

22

JUANA. Hard work never killed anybody.

GALLO. Ay, mujer! Can't you think what you've done, you bowed his head down.

JUANA. What was I suppose to do? There ain't no other work here. I can't see anything wrong with it for a little while.

GALLO. The difference between them and us, is we never put a foot into the fields. We stayed independent — we worked for nobody. They have to respect us, to respect our roosters. *(Hector and Adan enter. They are both very dirty. Hector has Zapata, in his carrier. Adan has a carrier containing a second rooster. Gallo and Hector stare at each other.)* Well ... you are taller. This offshoot ... this little bud has grown.

HECTOR. Yeah, well ... that must be why you seem ... smaller.

GALLO. Un abrazo!

HECTOR. I'm dirty. I'm sweaty.

GALLO. I see that.

HECTOR. I'm afraid I smell of the fields.

GALLO. Yes.

HECTOR. Of cheap abundant peon labor ... the scent would gag you.

GALLO. It's going to kill you.

HECTOR. Mama says hard work never killed anyone ... isn't that right, Mother?

JUANA. It's only for a little while. Your papa thinks that—

GALLO. I'll tell him what I think. Now what about those tamales you promised me?

JUANA. Ah sí, con permiso ... I got some work in the kitchen.

ADAN. Oh sí, Mrs. Juana, los tamales ... que rico.

JUANA. *(Smiling at Adan.)* I hope they're the kind you like. *(She exits into house.)*

GALLO. Hijo, you always take the bird with you into the fields?

HECTOR. No, not always.

GALLO. This bird has to look like he's got secrets ... no one but us should be familiar with him.

23

HECTOR. This is Adan.

ADAN. Es un honor, Mr. El Gallo. *(Angela sticks her head out from under the house. Adan and Gallo shake hands and greet each other.)*

GALLO. *(Referring to Zapata.)* Let him out ... he needs a bigger carrier ... he's a flyer.

ADAN. Como Filipino birds?

GALLO. Yes but this baby boy he's got a surprise. He's got a kick.

ADAN. Like Cuban bird?

GALLO. He'll fight in the air, he'll fight on the ground. You can put spurs or razors on that kick and he'll cut any bird to ribbons. You can put money on that.

ADAN. Hijo! Señor ... how you know? He never fight. Maybe he only kick in cage.

GALLO. I know because I'm his papa ... *(Pointing to the other carrier.)* That your bird?

ADAN. Sí, pero no good ... no fight. San Juan, he run away.

GALLO. I'll make him fight. Just let him out.

ADAN. Mr. El Gallo, you give this pendejo bird too much honor. Gracias Señor, pero this poor bird, he no can fight.

GALLO. Is it the bird, or you who will not fight?

HECTOR. The bird is too young. He doesn't want him to fight.

GALLO. I've never seen a bird that won't fight, but there are men who are cowards.

HECTOR. He is not a coward.

ADAN. This is true, pero I am not El Gallo. In my country all men who love di rooster know Mr. El Gallo. They tell of di famoso día de los muertos fight in Jacinto Park.

GALLO. Ah, you heard about that fight. You remember that fight, Hector?

HECTOR. No.

GALLO. First time you saw a real cockfight ... Abuelo took you ... How could you forget your first cockfight? *(To Adan.)* Go on, take your bird out. I'll make him fight. *(Gallo takes a drink from a bottle, then blows on San Juan. As he does this, lights go down almost to black.*

*Pinspot comes up C. as other lights come up to a dark red. During this
process, we hear Gallo's voice — "Ready," then a few beats later "Pit!"
On this cue two dancer/roosters jump into the pinspot. This rooster dance
is savage. The dancers wear razors on their feet. The Zapata dancer
jumps very high. The poor San Juan dancer stays close to the ground.
Throughout the dance, we hear drums and foot-stomping. At every hit,
there is a big drum pound. During the fight, Hector appears on the
porch.)*

HECTOR. *(To himself.)* It was in Jacinto Park ... the crowd was a
monster, made up of individual human beings stuck together by
sweat and spittle. Their gaping mouths let out screams, curses, and
foul gases, masticating, smacking, eager for the kill. You stood up.
The monster roared. Quasimoto, your bird, in one hand. You lifted
him high, "Pit!" went the call. "Pit!" roared the monster. And you
threw him into the ring ... soaring with the blades on his heels flashing I heard the mighty rage of his wings and my heart soared with
him. He was a whirlwind flashing and slashing like a dark avenging
angel then like some distant rainbow star exploding he was hit. The
monster crowd inhaled, sucking back their hopes ... in that vacuum
he was pulled down. My heart went down the same dark shaft, my
brains slammed against the earth's hard crust ... my eyes clouded ...
my arteries gushed ... my lungs collapsed. "Get up," said Abuelo,
"up here with me, and you will see a miracle." You, Father, picked
up Quasimoto, a lifeless pile of bloody feathers, holding his head oh
so gently, you closed your eyes, and like a great wave receding, you
drew a breath that came from deep within your ocean floor. I heard
the stones rumble, the mountains shift, the topsoil move, and as
your breath slammed on the beaches, Quasimoto sputtered back to
life. Oh Papi, breathe on me. *(Angela appears and stands behind her
brother. Her wings are spread very far out. Drums and stomping cres-
cendo as Zapata brutally kills San Juan. Blackout.)*

ACT TWO

Scene 1

Early afternoon. The table is set up in the middle of the yard in a festive way, with tablecloth, flowers, a bowl of peaches, and bottles of whiskey and wine. Gallo is in the henhouse with Adan. Hector is in the bathroom, Juana and Chata are in the kitchen. Angela is by the little cemetery writing on a tombstone.

ANGELA.   Here lies Angela Ester Morales died of acute neglect. Although she is mourned by many, she goes to a far, far, better place, where they have better food. *(Angela slides under the house as Juana comes out wearing a fresh housedress and carrying a steaming pot.)*

JUANA.   *(Yelling.)* Hector! Angela! You kids wash up, it's time to eat. *(Juana hurries back into the house, almost knocking Chata down as she comes out with a tray of tortillas. she is heavily made up, wearing tight clothes, dangling earrings, high-heeled shoes. A cigarette dangles from her mouth.)*

CHATA.   Why are you eating out here?

JUANA.   He wants it. Says he don't wanta hide in the house.

CHATA.   Begging for trouble.

JUANA.   What can I do, he's the *man. (She goes into the house.)*

CHATA.   Ah, they're all shit! Just want trouble. Soup's on! *(Chata pours herself a quick shot of whiskey, shoots it down and makes a face. Juana comes out with another pot.)*

JUANA.   You better tell 'em that the food's ready. *(Chata goes to henhouse.)* Hector!

HECTOR. *(Coming out on porch.)* What?

JUANA. It's time to eat ... you look real nice honey. Makes me proud to have your papa see you all dressed up.

HECTOR. Okay. Okay. Don't make a big deal about it. I just don't want him to think—

JUANA. I just feel so happy—

HECTOR. I just don't want him to think—

JUANA. Hijito! You love your papa ... don't you?

HECTOR. Mother!

JUANA. I know you a little mad at him ... pero when he comes home it's like the sun when it—

HECTOR. Shshshsh! *(Chata, Gallo and Adan come out of the henhouse.)*

GALLO. We have to sharpen and polish those spurs. I want them to flash.

JUANA. *(To Gallo.)* The food's ready ... we fixed what you like ... mole, rice, frijolitos ... tamales.

GALLO. Tamales estilo Jalisco!

CHATA. *(Looking Hector over.)* Ay Papi que rico estás! *(Hector quickly sits down.)* Honey! You gonna have to beat all them women off with a stick, when they see you and that rooster tonight.

ADAN. No worry Hector, I be there ... down you mujeres, women leave de Mr. Hector and me alone ... Ay Mama! *(He has a giggling fit.)*

GALLO. *(Kissing Juana.)* It's wonderful to be in love ... to be touched by the noble fever.

CHATA. Ah, you're better off with a touch of typhoid.

JUANA. I ... gracias al Señor que ... my whole family is here. *(She looks around. She yells.)*

JUANA. Angela! Angie!

HECTOR. Mom!

JUANA. Where is she? Where is your sister?

HECTOR. Talking to the saints! I don't know. *(Juana gets up, goes to the spot where Angela slides under the house, gets down on her hands and knees and yells.)*

JUANA. Angela! Angela! You leave them saints alone. You hear

27

me! *(As everybody looks at Juana, Angela comes from behind the house and tiptoes toward the henhouse. Hector is the only one to see her. Using hand signals, she pleads to him to be quiet. Juana peers under the house.)* Angie! Honey ... your mama worked for days to fix this food and now it's getting cold. *(To Gallo.)* You should see how sweet she looks when she's all dressed up. *(To under the house.)* You ain't got no manners ... ain't even said hello to your father. *(To Gallo.)* She prays a lot ... and she's got real pretty eyes.

CHATA. *(To Gallo.)* She's sorta ... the bashful type ... you know.

JUANA. *(To Gallo.)* And she ain't spoiled.

CHATA. *(Taking a drink.)* Nah, all them kids smell like that.

JUANA. *(To under the house.)* Angie!

GALLO. Juana leave her alone.

JUANA. Okay. Angie, I'm gonna ignore you, 'cause you spoiled my day, this day that I been looking forward to for years and years and now you making me look like a bad mama, what's your papa gonna think of us.

GALLO. Juana, she'll come out when she's ready. *(Juana goes back to the table.)*

CHATA. Maybe was them roosters fighting got her scared.

ADAN. Poor San Juan.

GALLO. Adan, drink up and I'll see you get one of our famous Champion Morales birds.

HECTOR. What famous Champion Morales birds?

GALLO. The ones I paid for dearly, the ones I came home to raise ... isn't that right mi amor?

JUANA. Yes ... you see honey your papa's gonna stay home ... raise birds ... I think Abuelo would want that.

GALLO. And after they see our bird tonight ... see first I want them to think it's just you and the bird up there. And the bets are down, I'll take over and they're gonna know we got roosters. A toast ... *(As Gallo stands up, everybody raises a glass, except Hector. Angela tiptoes from the henhouse carrying Zapata. She goes behind and under the house. Only Hector sees her.)* To the finest fighting cocks ever to be seen. *(He slides bottle to Hector.)*

HECTOR. *(Sliding the bottle back.)* No. *(Pause.)*

GALLO. Too good to drink with your old man.

HECTOR. I only drink with people I trust.

CHATA. Me ... I drink with anybody. Maybe that's my problem.

GALLO. I am your father.

CHATA. I like it better when I drink alone. Ya meet a better class of people that way.

HECTOR. But it's my bird. Abuelo left it to me.

GALLO. Abuelo was my father, and you are my son. I see no problem. Now let's eat.

HECTOR. Mother!

JUANA. Let's eat, honey, and we can talk about it later.

ADAN. Ay the mole muy delicious ... the mole muy rico ... the cole muy beautiful y Mrs. Juana. Today, you look beautiful, like the mole.

GALLO. Hm, sabroso, exquisto.

JUANA. I bet you been in plenty of fancy places got better food than this.

GALLO. This is home cooking, I know that your hands made it ... These ... these are the hands of a beautiful woman...

HECTOR. Ha! Bullshit.

GALLO. We say your mother is beautiful and you call it bullshit? I find that very disrespectful.

JUANA. Hijo, you're right ... it's just the way people talk, I know I ain't beautiful.

ADAN. Sí, muy beautiful.

GALLO. Ya ves! ... If your son doesn't have the eyes, the soul, the imagination to see it ... it's his loss.

HECTOR. That's right. I just can't seem to stretch my imagination that far.

GALLO. This is an insult to your mother.

HECTOR. It's the truth. That is a plain, tired, worn-out woman.

GALLO. Shut up.

HECTOR. The hands of a beautiful woman! Those aren't hands,

29

they're claws because she has to scratch for her living.

JUANA. Please, Hector, let him say what he wants ... I know I ain't beautiful. It don't go to my head.

HECTOR. But it goes to your heart which is worse. Did he ever really take care of you? Did he ever go out and work to put food on the table, to buy you a dress? All he has is words, and he throws a few cheap words to you and you come to life. Don't you have any pride?

GALLO. Your mother has great courage to trust and believe in me.

HECTOR. Stupidity!

GALLO. You know nothing!

HECTOR. You don't seem to realize that it is my rooster. And that after the fight, depending on the outcome, I will sell him or eat him. I have made a deal with the Filipinos.

JUANA. Ay Hector! You've spoiled everything. All this food ... I worked so hard ... for this day.

GALLO. You're not selling anything to anybody. This is nothing to joke about.

HECTOR. I don't want to spend my life training chickens to be better killers. And I don't want to spend my whole life in this valley. Mother, Aunt Chata, excuse me.

CHATA. Ah? ... O sí hijo pase ... sometimes Hector can be a real gentleman. *(Hector starts to leave.)*

GALLO. Son! ... You have no courage, no juice ... you are a disgrace to me.

JUANA. Ay, Gallo don't say that to him.

HECTOR. Do you think I care what you think ... Father.

JUANA. Hijo no ... for me just once for me. I don't wanna be alone no more.

HECTOR. What about me? You have me, you'll always have me, I'll work, I've always worked, I can take care of you. I won't leave you.

JUANA. It ain't the same, honey.

HECTOR. Yeah ... He comes first for you, he will always come first.

GALLO. If you sell that bird, it will be over your dead body.

HECTOR. You can't stop me. *(Exit Hector. Chata takes a plate of food and bowl of peaches to the under-the-house area and tries to tempt Angela out.)*

GALLO. He doesn't seem to realize ... coward ... too bad. *(Gallo goes to the henhouse. Juana starts to follow him.)*

JUANA. Talk to him ... he's a good boy ... if you just talk ... *(Seeing Adan still eating.)* Is it good? You really like it?

ADAN. Hm! Sabroso!

CHATA. Come on Angie ... it's real good. *(Gallo returns running.)*

GALLO. He's gone ... the bird is gone...

ADAN. Yo no see nada, nada.

JUANA. He'll bring it back, he's a good boy. He's just a little upset ... you know.

GALLO. Nobody fools with my roosters. Not even this over-petted, over-pampered viper you spawned. Go and pray to your Dark Virgin. You know what I'm capable of. *(Exit Gallo. Adan stops eating and tries to comfort Juana as she puts her head down on the table and cries.)*

ADAN. No cry, no cry Mrs. Juana. Di women cry y Adan, he not know what to do. *(Juana cries louder.)* Ay Mrs. Juana, for sure di flowers will die ... di trees will be torn from di ground, freshness will leave di morning, softness will leave di night ... *(Juana's cries increase.)* Ay Dios! *(From his pocket, he brings out the letter Angela wrote for him. He crosses himself.)* Mrs. di Juana ... *(Reading with great difficulty.)* Di ... impulses ... of my ... heart ... are such ... *(Throwing letter aside.)* A que la fregada! Mrs. Juana, Adan have mucho amor for you. My heart break to see you cry. I will not a breathe. When you no cry then I will breathe. *(Adan takes a big breath and holds it. Slowly Juana stops crying and lifts her head. Adan, suffering some discomfort, continues to hold his breath.)*

JUANA. I been dreaming. Nothing's gonna change. I gotta face facts. *(Adan let his breath out in a great whoosh. Angela pops out from under the house and takes a peach from Chata's hand. She stares at the peach with great intensity.)*

31

CHATA. Angie, ain't it nice to have the family all together again?

ANGELA. There is no pit in this peach. It is hollow. Instead of the pit, there is a whole little world, a little blue-green crystal-clear ocean, with little schools of tiny darting silver fish. On a tiny rock sits a mermaid with little teenie-weenie kinky yellow hair. A tiny sun is being pulled across a little china-blue sky by teenie-weenie white horses with itty-bitty wings. There is an island with tiny palm trees and tiny thatched hut. Next to the hut stand a tiny man and woman. She is wearing flowers and leaves. He is wearing one single leaf. On their heads are little bitty halos. In their arms is a little bitsy baby. He isn't wearing anything.

CHATA. Let me see ... *(Looking at peach.)* I can't see dick! *(Blackout.)*

Scene 2

Later in the afternoon. Chata sits on the porch steps, her legs spread out, fanning herself. Juana sits on a straight-back chair, her hands folded on her lap. She rocks herself softly. She watches Angela, who is sitting on the ground drawing circles in the dirt, humming softly in time to her circles. The circles get deeper and deeper.

CHATA. It's hot ... I am waiting for a cool breeze...

ANGELA. Uh ha uh ha uh ha uh haa.

CHATA. Aire fresco ... come on cool breeze, come right over here.

ANGELA. Uh ha uh ha uh haa.

CHATA. Women! We're always waiting. *(Angela hums for a beat, then there is silence for a beat.)*

JUANA. It's because I'm so plain.

CHATA. Ah, you just work too much.

JUANA. Plainness runs in my family. My mother was plain, my grandmother was plain, my great-grandmother—

CHATA. It was the hard times ... the hard work that did it.

JUANA. My Aunt Chona was the plainest.

CHATA. I don't remember her.

JUANA. The one with the crossed eyes and the little mustache.

CHATA. Ay, Juanita, that woman had a beautiful soul, sewing those little tiny outfits for the statues of the saints. That woman was a saint.

JUANA. She's the one told on you that time you was drinking beer with them sailors at the cockfight.

CHATA. Disgusting old bitch! *(Angela hums for a beat as she continues drawing circles.)*

JUANA. I get up at six, I brush my teeth, no creams, no lotions, what they gonna do for me? I work that's all. I take care of people and I work. People look at me, they know that's all I do. I ain't got no secrets. No hidden gardens. I keep busy that's what I do. Don't stop, that's what I say to myself. Don't stop, 'cause you're not pretty enough, exciting enough, smart enough to just stand there.

ANGELA. Mama, I don't wanna be plain.

CHATA. Honey, you're too colorful to be plain.

ANGELA. Yeah, that's what I thought.

CHATA. Your mama forgets ... those years when her heart was filled with wild dreams when she use to weave little white star jasmine vines in her hair and drive all the men crazy.

JUANA. It ain't true ... she was the one always getting me in trouble.

CHATA. I wasn't the one they called Juanita la Morenita Sabrosita.

JUANA. Oh, Chata. We was young girls together ... in the summer, at Jacinto Park ... cockfights, fistfights, the music. At night we would jump out of our bedroom windows in our party dresses. With our good shoes in one hand, our hearts in the other, we ran barefoot through the wet grass, above us all the stars twinkling go, go, go.

CHATA. Nothing could stop us ... we had such a short time being girls.

33

JUANA. Now, all I am is an old hag.

CHATA. It ain't true.

JUANA. Sí, it's true enough. I carry burdens, I hang sheets, I scrub, I gather, I pick up, "Here sit down," "I'll wash it," "Here's fifty cents," "Have my chair," "Take my coat," "Here's a piece of my own live flesh"!

CHATA. Es la menopause, that's what it is. You getting it early. I knew this woman once, use to pull out her hair.

JUANA. I don't care, I don't want any stories, I don't care what happens to Fulano Mangano ... I just wanna stand still, I wanna be interesting, exciting enough to stand still.

CHATA. Ay, mujer!

JUANA. And I want to look like I got secrets.

CHATA. Juana!

JUANA. Don't call me Juana. Juana is a mule's name.

CHATA. Ah, you're crazy! That new gray hen, the kids named her Juana. See, they think of you.

JUANA. A gray hen! An old gray hen, that's all I am. An old gray hen in a family of roosters. No more! I want feathers, I wanna strut, too. I wanna crow.

ANGELA. Mama!

JUANA. Don't! Don't call me Mama. I am not Mama ... I am ... I am that movie star, that famous dancer and heartbreaker "Morenita Sabrosita" ... and now if my fans will excuse me I'm gonna take a bath in champagne, eat cherry bonbons and paint my toenails. *(She goes into house.)*

CHATA. *(To Juana.)* We got champagne? *(Chata goes into the house as Angela goes to the little cemetery and puts up a new tombstone.)*

ANGELA. *(Printing on tombstone.)* Here lies Juana Morales. Beloved Wife of El Gallo, Blessed Mother to Angela and Horrible Hector. Died of acute identity crisis sustained during la menopause.

34

Scene 3

Lights go down, as Angela sits on her box/table at the little cemetery. The long shadows of men fall on Angela and the cemetery.

SHADOW #1. There's that spooky kid. You go brother.

SHADOW #2. Ah, it's just a weird kid. Hey! You! Kid! *(Angela does not acknowledge them.)*

SHADOW #1. Call her "Angel."

SHADOW #2. Hey, Angel. *(Angela looks up.)*

SHADOW #1. See what I mean.

SHADOW #2. Listen kid, tell your old man, we got business to discuss.

SHADOW #1. Yeah, and you make sure he gets the message.

ANGELA. My old man, my Holy Father, my all powerful Father, sees no problems. If there are problems, I am the angel of this yard. I am the comet. I am the whirlwind. I am the shooting stars. Feel my vibrance.

SHADOW #1. I feel it, right behind my ears, like ... like ...

ANGELA. Locust wings.

SHADOW #1. Let's get outta here.

SHADOW #2. Tell Gallo some pals dropped by to settle an old score.

SHADOW #1. Come on!

SHADOW #2. *(Voice trailing off.)* Hey! That kid don't scare me, see.

SHADOW #1. *(Voice trailing off.)* I'm telling ya, my ears hurt. *(Exit shadows. Lights go back up. Angela folds her hands in prayer.)*

ANGELA. Holy Father, please help me, I feel the illumination, the fever of grace slipping away. I need to know that you are with me, that you take an interest in my concerns. Send me a little demonstration, a sign. Any sign ... I don't care. Stigmata, visions, voices, send an angel, burn a bush ... I am attracted to levitation ... but you choose ... I'll just lay here and wait. *(Angela lies down on the ground waiting. After a few beats Hector enters. He slowly walks up to Angela and looks down on her for a beat.)*

HECTOR. What are you doing?

ANGELA. *(Sitting up.)* Ohhh ... you're no sign.

HECTOR. What is going on?

ANGELA. Weird, shady men came here looking for Gallo. Two of them. They were not polite.

HECTOR. I see ... So your reaction is to lay stretched out on the dirt instead of going into the house.

ANGELA. Hector, please, I am scared ... I wanted a sign. *(Hector sits down next to Angela.)*

HECTOR. Hey, you're the shooting-star woman, you can't be scared.

ANGELA. I am scared. Really scared. If I grow up will I still be scared? Are grown-ups scared?

HECTOR. Always scared, trembling ... cowering ... this ... this second, now ... this planet that we are sitting on is wobbling precariously on its lightning path around the sun and every second the sun is exploding ... stars are shooting at us from deep distant space, comets zoom around us, meteor rocks are being hurled through distances we measure in light ... this very earth which we call our home, our mother, has catastrophic moods, she keeps moving mountains, receding like an overburdened beast trying to shake off ... Life is violent.

ANGELA. You're scared about the fight ... huh?

HECTOR. No. Whatever happens, Papi will still only care about the rooster. That's his son, that's who gets it all.

ANGELA. Maybe if we gave him the rooster he'd stay here and be happy.

HECTOR. He has to stay for us not the rooster ... Angela ... you ... you were great taking the rooster.

ANGELA. He kept killing the little chicks. How could he do that Hector? He's their papa.

HECTOR. Training. Look Angela, you're the angel of this yard. You keep a close guard on that rooster. Don't let anyone near him... promise me.

ANGELA. Yes.

HECTOR. That's a real promise now. No crossed fingers behind your back.

ANGELA. I promise already. *(She spreads her hands out in front of her, then kisses the tip of her thumb.)* May God strike me dumb, make me a plain whiny person and take away my gift of faith. Forever and ever, throughout my mortal years on earth, and throughout the everlasting fires of hell. Amen. Satisfied?

HECTOR. Yes.

ANGELA. Gee, maybe I should have given myself a little leeway, a little room for error. *(Chata enters from the house with a bottle and glass.)*

HECTOR. Too late now. Can't take it back.

CHATA. Oh, oh, look who's here. Angie, your mama needs some cheering up, a nice hug, an angel's kiss, maybe a little song.

ANGELA. Litany to the Virgin. That's her favorite. *(She exits.)*

CHATA. Men are shit. Pure shit.

HECTOR. And you're still drinking.

CHATA. Stay outta my drinking. You hurt your mama, Hector.

HECTOR. Too bad.

CHATA. Ay Dios, what a man he is now.

HECTOR. Yeah, well what about you? Didn't you break Abuelo's heart when you became a whore?

CHATA. They called me the encyclopedia of love. You want to turn a few pages? Your Aunt Chata could show you a few things.

HECTOR. You're disgusting.

CHATA. Is that what fascinates, you, honey? Is that why I always find you peeping at me, mirrors at the keyhole, your eyeballs in the cracks, spying when I'm sleeping, smelling my kimono.

37

HECTOR. You're drunk.

CHATA. I ain't drunk, honey.

HECTOR. You drink too much. It's not ... good for you ... it makes you ugly.

CHATA. Ain't none of your business. Don't tell me what to do Hector.

HECTOR. I have to, it's for your own good.

CHATA. You got nothing to say about it, you ain't my man, and you ain't your mama's man. The sooner you learn that the better ... take your bird, leave it, eat or sell it, but get out of here. *(Hector stands alone in the yard, as Chata goes to the door. She turns. They look at each other.)* What are you hanging around here for? Go on! Get out! It ain't your home anymore. *(Chata takes a broom and shoos Hector from the yard.)* Shoo! Shoo! You don't belong here, it ain't your place anymore.

HECTOR. Stop it, stop it, stop it. *(Hector goes to the outside boundary of the yard, where he falls to his knees and buries his face in his hands, as Chata comes slowly up behind him.)*

CHATA. I feel like I'm tearing my own flesh from my bones ... He's back. Honey, we got too many roosters in this yard.

HECTOR. Did you sleep with my father? Did he yearn for you as you slept in your little white, chaste, narrow bed? Did he steal you when you were dreaming?

CHATA. *(Embracing him.)* Shshsh...

HECTOR. I'm not like him.

CHATA. You're just like him, so handsome you make my teeth ache.

HECTOR. Whore, mother, sister, saint-woman, moon-woman, give me the shelter of your darkness. fold me like a fan and take me into your stillness, submerge me beneath the mysteries, baptize me, bear me up, give me life, breathe on me. *(Chata enfolds him as the lights fade. We hear Angela reciting the litany.)*

ANGELA. *(Offstage.)* She is the Gate of Heaven, the Mystical Rose, the Flower of Consolation, the Fire of Transcendence, and the Queen of Love.

Scene 4

Lights come up to indicate that time has passed. Angela is alone in the yard. She sniffs the air.

ANGELA. Tres Rosas! *(Angela slides under the house as Gallo enters. He sees a brief flash of Angela from the corner of his eye. He walks slowly into the yard. He stops by the little cemetery and reads the tombstones. He feels the urge for a drink. He goes to the table and has a shot. He sits.)*

GALLO. Acute neglect? ... uh-huh ... I thought I felt a little spirit, slight, delicate ... yes I feel it. A little tenderness... a little greenness ... *(Examining the ground.)* What's this? Tracks ... little tiny paws ... there ... *(Following tracks.)* and there ... *(Gallo pretends to be following tracks to the porch. Then with one great leap he jumps in the opposite direction, surprising the hell out of Angela, and pulls her from under the house by her heels.)* Ah, ha!

ANGELA. Shit! Hey! You're ripping my wings! You shithead! Put me down! Don't touch me! *(Gallo puts Angela down, throws his hands up to indicate he won't touch her. They stand and stare at each other. Angela goes to the little cemetery, never taking her eyes off Gallo. They continue to stare for a beat, then Angela looks up to Heaven, slapping her hands together in prayer.)* There is a person here trying to con me, but I don't con that easy.

GALLO. *(Slapping his hands in prayer.)* There is a person here who swallows saints but defecates devils.

ANGELA. *(To Heaven.)* He comes here smelling of rosas using sweet oily words ... it's phony, its obnoxious, it's obscene ... I wanna throw up.

GALLO. I came here to see my baby, my little angel, my little woman of the shooting stars, my light delicate splendorous daughter. But she is as light, as delicate, as splendid as an angel's fart.

39

ANGELA. Angels do not fart. They do not have a digestive system. That's why they can all scrunch together on the head of a pin.

GALLO. Oh, ... I only come with my love—

ANGELA. *(Interrupting.)* You only came with words ... well, where were these words on my birthday, Christmas, my saint's day? Where's my Easter outfit, my trip to Disneyland, the orthodontist ... You owe me.

GALLO. Sweet Jesus ... What a monster! I owe you ... but Angela! Angela! Angela! How many times have I written that name on prison walls. On bits of paper, on the skin of my arms.

ANGELA. *(To Heaven.)* He's hopeless! You write everybody's name on your arms.

GALLO. Women like to know that they're on your flesh.

ANGELA. I am not a woman. I'm your baby daughter. You said so yourself.

GALLO. I'm afraid ... fathers to daughters ... that's so delicate. I don't know ... what to do ... help me Angela. How do I know what to do?

ANGELA. Instinct! Ain't ya got no instinct? Don't you feel anything?

GALLO. *(Moving closer to Angela.)* When you were a little baby, you were a miracle of tiny fingers and toes and dimples and you had a soft spot on the top of your head.

ANGELA. I still have it, see.

GALLO. I wanted to take you into my arms and crush you against my chest so that I could keep you forever and nobody, and nothing, could ever, ever hurt you because you would be safe ... my little offshoot, my little bud, my little flower growing inside my chest.

ANGELA. Papi...

GALLO. Sí, sí, hijita. Your papi's here.

ANGELA. And Papi these men come all the—

GALLO. *(Holding Angela.)* Shshsh ... it's nothing, nothing and you thought I forgot about you ... well it just hurt too much, do you understand?

40

ANGELA. You had to pull down some hard time and the only way to survive was to cut off all feelings and become an animal just like the rest of them.

GALLO. Well, something like that. Honey you know what I wish—

ANGELA. Papa, did the lights really go down when they put the people in the electric chair?

GALLO. Angela, what a ... Honey you know what I wish—

ANGELA. Did they force you to make license plates? Hector and I would look real close at the one that started with a G. We thought you made them. "What craftsmanship!" Hector used to say.

GALLO. Don't you have any normal interests?

ANGELA. Like what?

GALLO. Like swimming ... you know what I wish? That we could take a trip and see the ocean together.

ANGELA. I've never seen the ocean. When?

GALLO. Just you and me. Laying on our bellies, feeding the seagulls, riding the waves.

ANGELA. I can't swim.

GALLO. I will teach you, that's what fathers are for—

ANGELA. *(To Heaven.)* Angels and saints did you hear? My father's going to teach me to swim!

GALLO. Now Angela, I didn't promise.

ANGELA. But you said—

GALLO. I want to but I have to hurry and fix things. I have to find Hector, talk to him and find that rooster fast before Hector sells him. Honey you pray to St. Anthony, your prayers are powerful ... unless ... St. Anthony he listen to you?

ANGELA. *(Crossing her fingers.)* Hey, we're like that.

GALLO. Ask St. Anthony, Angela ... then we can go to the ocean.

ANGELA. Truly Papi? Just you and me? And will you stay with us forever and ever?

GALLO. Wild horses couldn't drag me away.

ANGELA. Close your eyes. Tony! Tony! Look around, Zapata's lost and can't be found. *(She goes under the house, gets Zapata, and*

41

gives him to Gallo.) I found him Papi, he was—

GALLO. Ya lindo, ya. *(To bird.)* Papa's got you now. Angela you keep quiet now honey, this is our secret.

ANGELA. What about Hector?

GALLO. I'm going to talk to Hector now. You go inside and get all dressed up. So I can be proud of my girl. I'll pick you up after the fight. *(He exits.)*

ANGELA. Your girl! *(Singing.)* We are going to the ocean, we are going to the sea, we are going to the ocean to see what we can see ... *(Angela goes into the house. We hear cha-cha music.)*

CHATA. *(Offstage.)* One, two ... not like that ... I'm getting tired ... what time's *Zorro* on?

JUANA. No, no ... Just one more. *(Singing.)* Cha, cha, cha, que rico, ... cha, cha, cha ... Ay, I could do it all night. *(Enter Gallo running, breathing hard. He has Zapata's carrier. He goes to the door and yells.)*

GALLO. Juana! Juana! *(Juana and Chata come to the door.)* I need money ... and my stuff. I gotta leave ... something's come up ... Do you hear me? I need money now.

JUANA. I hear ya ... you ain't even been here a day and already you're gone ... nothing's going to change with you ... nothing. I was having fun, dancing, remembering old times, do you know how long—

GALLO. I don't have time for this, just give me the money.

JUANA. I ain't got any!

CHATA. I got some. *(She goes in the house.)*

GALLO. The Filipino, somebody told him about the bird. Oh, ya, ya my little hen, don't you ruffle those pretty feathers, I'll be back.

JUANA. No, you always gonna be running.

GALLO. If it was just me, I'd stay. You know that, Juana? You know I'd stay, but I got the bird to think of, gotta hide him, breed him good, soon as I get some good stags I'll come home ... this is just a little setback. *(Chata returns with suitcase and money.)*

JUANA. You know how long it's been since I went dancing?

CHATA. Here, you're gona need this. *(Give him the suitcase.)* And

42

this is all the cash I got. *(Angela enters as Gallo counts the money. She is dressed in a red strapless dress made tight by large visible safety pins, high heels, and a great deal of heavy makeup and jewelry. The effect is one of a young girl dressed like a tart for a costume party. She carries a suitcase, purse and her donation can.)*

GALLO. Is this all you got?

ANGELA. *(Shaking the can.)* Don't worry Papa, I got my donation-can money. *(They all stare at her for a beat.)*

JUANA & CHATA. Angela?!!

JUANA. Angie, you got on your mama's old party dress.

CHATA. Yeah, and all my jewelry ... where you going?

ANGELA. Papa, didn't you hear me? I have money. *(She shakes the can.)*

GALLO. Oh honey, don't you look pretty ... now you got a little bit too much lipstick on, let your mama wipe some off.

ANGELA. Are we leaving now?

JUANA. Gallo!

GALLO. Shshsh Juana ... Angela, I gotta talk to your mama for a few minutes. You go in the house and I'll come and get you.

ANGELA. Are you sure?

GALLO. Don't you trust me, Angie?

CHATA. Come on Angie, I'll show you how to draw eyebrows. First you draw a straight line across your forehead and then spit on your finger and rub out the middle. Let's go in and try it.

ANGELA. Really, Aunt Chata, I'm not a child, you don't have to patronize me.

CHATA. Okay, I'll give you the lowdown on blow-jobs. *(Angela and Chata exit into the house.)* Now, don't tell your mama...

GALLO. Juana, keep her in the house until I leave.

JUANA. You promised to take her with you?

GALLO. I had to get the bird. I said I would take her to the ocean.

JUANA. Ay bruto! How could you do it?

GALLO. How was I to know this would happen ... and Juanita, it hurts me to say this but that kid is crazy...

JUANA. No, no señor, she is not crazy and I ain't gonna let you call

43

her crazy. She got the spirit they broke in me. I ain't gonna let it happen to her.

GALLO. Shshsh! Don't get so excited. It isn't important.

JUANA. It's important ... it's her spirit, her soul and you ain't gonna stomp on it ... you hear me. *(Adan enters running.)*

ADAN. Mr. El Gallo ... bad men! Mucho bad, y mucho ugly. Looking for you y Zapata. All ober they look for you ... You leave Mr. El Gallo. You go far away. I take you. I go for my truck.

GALLO. You are a good friend Adan, and my new partner.

ADAN. Oh, thank you Mr. El Gallo. I am proud. But is better I come back here to Mrs. Juana y Hector.

JUANA. Thank you, Adan.

GALLO. We better hurry.

ADAN. Sí, sí, I come back with truck. *(He exits. Juana goes into the house. Hector enters as Gallo starts to pack his suitcase.)*

HECTOR. *(Seeing Zapata.)* You must have really sold her a bill of goods to get Zapata.

GALLO. Look, there's trouble ... the Filipino send you?

HECTOR. No, how could you think I would work for him, but I came to get Zapata.

GALLO. You're the one told him about the bird.

HECTOR. Yes. I made a deal with the Filipino. He'll leave you alone if I give him the rooster.

GALLO. That's a lie and you fell for it.

HECTOR. No, he is an honorable man, we were here unprotected for seven years and he never bothered us. It's his bird, Papi.

GALLO. No, I paid seven years of my life for this baby.

HECTOR. And he lost his son. It's the right thing to do. *(A truck horn is heard. Angela comes out of the house with her suitcase, Juana and Chata follow after her.)*

ANGELA. Papa? Are we leaving now, Papa?

JUANA. Angie! No!

HECTOR. So that's it ... Angela, get back in the house.

ANGELA. I'm going with him, Hector.

HECTOR. Get back in the house, nobody's going anywhere.

44

ANGELA. No! I don't have to listen to you anymore. You're not my father.

JUANA. Angie ... he's not going to the ocean ... he can't take you. *(We hear the sound of Adan's truck. The horn is heard as Gallo starts backing away, picking up Zapata's carrier.)*

ANGELA. Papi, wait for me! Papa, you promised.

GALLO. You're all grown up now, you don't need your old man.

CHATA. Hector! *(Gallo turns, tries to run out. Angela grabs him, knocking Zapata's carrier out of his hand. Hector picks up the carrier.)*

ANGELA. No Papa, we need you and Mama needs you, we've been waiting, and waiting, you can't leave, you promised.

JUANA. They'll kill you Gallo.

GALLO. *(Throwing Angela off.)* Stop sucking off me. I got nothing for you.

ANGELA. *(Beating her fists on the ground.)* No, no, Papa! You promised me! ... Oh, Hector ... No, no, I promised Hector. *(Drums begin as punctuation of the pounding of Angela's fists on the ground. Lights change. A special on Angela and another on Gallo and Hector come up, as shadows appear. Angela sees shadows.)* Ah ... Holy Father, Abuelo.

GALLO. *(To Hector.)* Give me that bird.

ANGELA. Saints, Angels, Mama.

JUANA. *(Trying to pick up Angela.)* Come on Angie, get up.

GALLO. *(To Hector.)* What do you want?

HECTOR. You, alive, Papi.

CHATA. Careful, Hector.

ANGELA. I've lost my faith. I am splintered.

GALLO. *(Imitating Hector.)* You Papi ... Give me life ... Make me a man. *(He whips out his stiletto.)* This is how you become a man. *(The drums get louder. We hear howling.)* Come on baby boy, show Daddy whatcha got.

JUANA. Are you crazy! That's your son!

ANGELA. I am cast down! Exiled! *(Gallo stalks Hector as drums follow their movements.)*

JUANA. Oh Gallo, you're killing your own children.

CHATA. Move Hector, don't think, move!

GALLO. Oh yeah, mi lindo, you like to fight ... eh?

JUANA. No, stop them! Please, please stop this.

ANGELA. Fallen from the light, condemned to the mud, to the shadows.

GALLO. You gotta learn baby boy.

CHATA. Look at him Hector. He's getting old, his hand is shaking ... take the knife! Stay down old warrior. Stay down.

ANGELA. Alone and diminished. This loneliness is unendurable.

JUANA. Hector!

HECTOR. Do I have it? Is this what you want me to be...

ANGELA. *(Looking to Heaven.)*

My brains are slammed against the earth's hard crust.

My eyes are clouded

My arteries gush

My lungs collapsed.

HECTOR. *(Letting go of Gallo.)* No! I am your son. *(Drums and cries stop.)*

ANGELA. Holy Father, Abuelo, Hector, breathe on me. *(Celestial sound as a white narrow shaft of light falls on Angela. She levitates, her wings spreading. Only Chata and Juana see this.)*

HECTOR. *(Taking a deep breath.)* Oh sweet air! *(He gets the rooster and sees Angela.)* Angela!

ADAN. *(Rushing in.)* I am here, I have truck ... *(Seeing Angela, he crosses himself.)* Ay Dios. *(He kneels.)*

JUANA. *(At Gallo's side.)* Gallo look!

GALLO. Did you see the hands on that kid, just like steel, never seen finer hands ... *(Seeing Angela.)* Sweet Jesus, my beautiful monster. *(He crosses himself.)*

CHATA. No, it ain't true.

HECTOR. *(Standing before Angela holding the rooster.)* Oh sweet hummingbird woman, shooting star, my comet, you are launched.

ANGELA. Abuelo, Queen of Heaven, All the Saints, All the Angels. It is true, I am back. I am restored. I am ... Hector, take me with you.

46

HECTOR. Everywhere ... Over the mountains, up to the stars.

ANGELA. To the very edge.

ADAN. Hector! Angelita! You take Adan. *(He goes to Angela.)*

CHATA. *(Looking at Angela.)* Shit happens ... been happening all my life, that's all I know.

JUANA. *(Holding Gallo like the Pieta.)* We seen it Gallo, with our own eyes.

ANGELA. *(To Hector and Adan.)* And I want my doorstep heaped with floral offering ... and *(Hector, Adan and Angela freeze. Chata removes the flower from her hair and holds it in her hand, trying to decide what to do. She freezes.)*

GALLO. Ay Juanaita, I had a vision of a hard-kicking flyer ... *(He yawns.)* the ultimate bird, noble, fino. *(He falls asleep. Juana looks at Gallo, smiles, then looks out half-smiling.)*

END OF PLAY

PROPERTY LIST

ACT I

SCENE 1

ONSTAGE
Chicken-wire henhouse
Miniature cemetery
Bare desert tree with low scratchy branches

OFFSTAGE
Suitcase (Gallo)
Switchblade stiletto (Gallo)

SCENE 2

ONSTAGE
Table
Chairs

OFFSTAGE
Cigarette (Chata)
Bowl containing balls of tortilla dough (Chata)

SCENE 3

ONSTAGE
Wings
White box containing:
 Cardboard tombstones
 Paper and crayons
 Writing tablet
 Pen
Collection can

2 dolls (dressed in nuns' habits; 1 has round sunglasses)
Doll's teapot and cup
Food
Letter

OFFSTAGE
Traveling carrier (Hector and Adan)
Coins (Adan)

SCENE 4
ONSTAGE
Bottle

OFFSTAGE
2nd traveling carrier (Adan)

ACT II

SCENE 1
ONSTAGE
Tablecloth
Flowers
Bowl of peaches
Bottles of whiskey and wine

OFFSTAGE
Steaming pot (Juana)
Tray of tortillas (Chata)
Cigarette (Chata)

SCENE 3
OFFSTAGE
Bottle and glass (Chata)
Suitcase (Chata)
Money (Chata)
Suitcase, purse, and collection can (Angela)

HEN HOUSE

HOUSE

PORCH

TREE AND
LITTLE CEMETERY

SCENE DESIGN
"ROOSTERS"